THE FIGURE 8 VOYAGE

**FIVE OCEANS, THREE CONTINENTS,
ONE YEAR, SOLO**

RANDALL REEVES

This book is for Jo, to whom all voyages return.

14 | A SECOND CHANCE

28 | OVER THE BOUNDING MAIN

48 | THE LONG, SLOW CLIMB

60 | THE NORTHWEST PASSAGE

86 | HOMECOMING

Contents

Design and layout: **www.stewart2.com**

Fetchamark Publications
Oakland | Ushuaia | Hobart | Halifax

For inquiries and orders please visit
www.figure8voyage.com

JAN 26
Gale

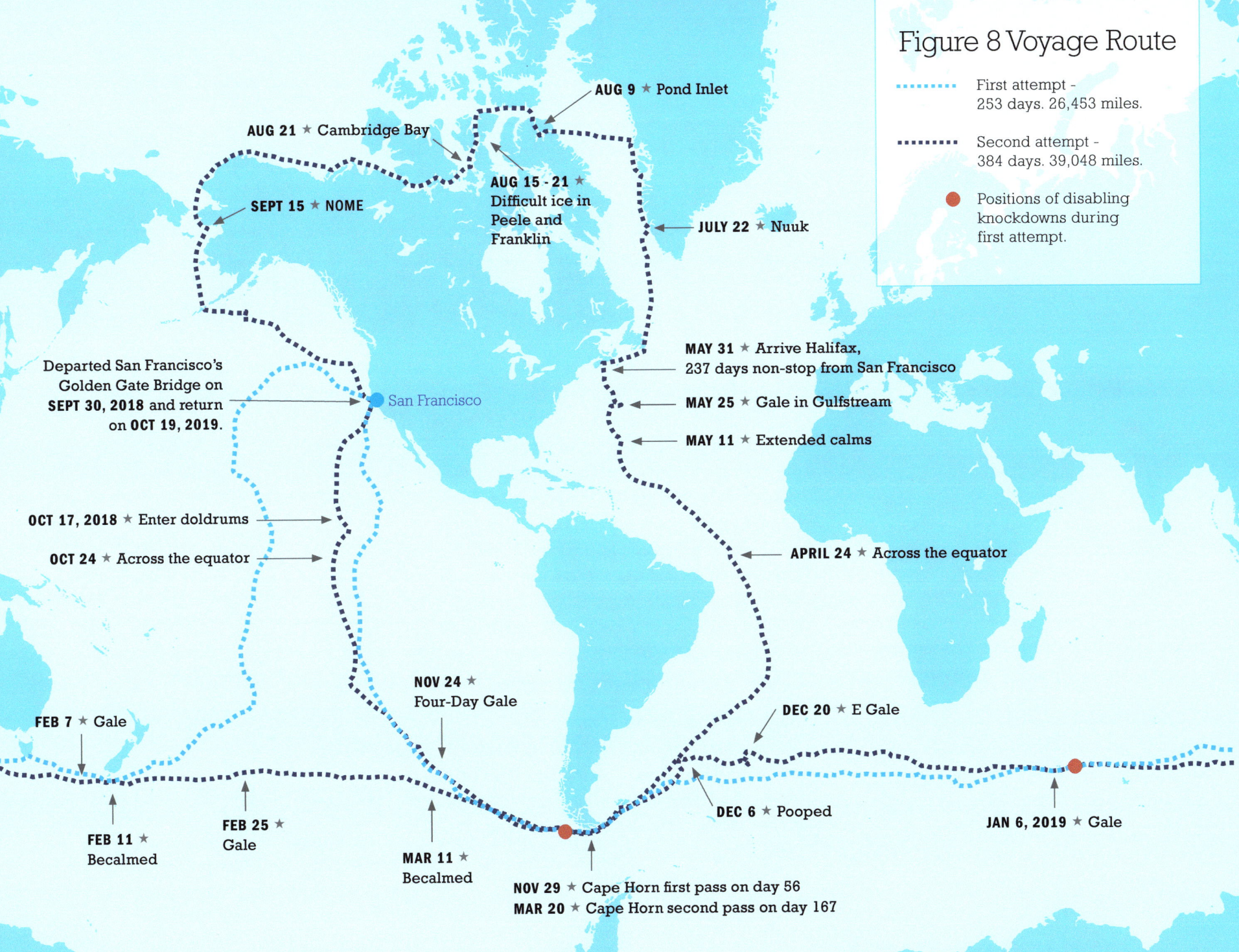

Figure 8 Voyage Route

First attempt - 253 days. 26,453 miles.

Second attempt - 384 days. 39,048 miles.

Positions of disabling knockdowns during first attempt.

AUG 9 ★ Pond Inlet

AUG 21 ★ Cambridge Bay

AUG 15 - 21 ★ Difficult ice in Peele and Franklin

SEPT 15 ★ NOME

JULY 22 ★ Nuuk

MAY 31 ★ Arrive Halifax, 237 days non-stop from San Francisco

MAY 25 ★ Gale in Gulfstream

MAY 11 ★ Extended calms

Departed San Francisco's Golden Gate Bridge on SEPT 30, 2018 and return on OCT 19, 2019.

San Francisco

OCT 17, 2018 ★ Enter doldrums

OCT 24 ★ Across the equator

APRIL 24 ★ Across the equator

NOV 24 ★ Four-Day Gale

DEC 20 ★ E Gale

FEB 7 ★ Gale

FEB 11 ★ Becalmed

FEB 25 ★ Gale

MAR 11 ★ Becalmed

DEC 6 ★ Pooped

JAN 6, 2019 ★ Gale

NOV 29 ★ Cape Horn first pass on day 56

MAR 20 ★ Cape Horn second pass on day 167

Introduction

Why a Picture Book?

As a young admirer of sea-faring stories, I was often most attracted to the pictures. Melville's *Moby Dick* may well have been written for boys, but this boy spent his hours in that volume admiring Rockwell Kent's woodcuts more than the sentences they were intended to illustrate.

As an adult, I have come to the end of many a bluewater tale—be it *Alone through the Roaring Forties, The Fight of the Firecrest, Once is Enough, The Long Way, A World of My Own, Ice with Everything*—having been captivated by the weave of words but wanting more than the scant few photographs at the book's center. What is the color of ocean that dances beneath Pacific trades? How does a wave curl and crash at 47 degrees south? What did *Joshua* really look like in a seaway?

The goal of this book, then, is to be a pictorial accompaniment to the longer Figure 8 Voyage narrative and to satisfy the person who, like me, may desire that additional perspective of a seagoing adventure story. Words here have been kept to a minimum and serve simply to frame the action and add context to the images. What's important is that the reader see the ocean as the camera sees it over many days, many miles and many latitudes.

What is the Figure 8 Voyage?

Simply put, this project combined into a single voyage two famously difficult ocean passages whose overall shape on the globe is the loops of a figure eight. One is the Clipper Route, which for hundreds of years connected Europe with Asia via the Great Capes, and the other is the long-sought but only recently accessible route through the Arctic, the Northwest Passage.

By now both routes have been completed by solo sailors in small boats, Francis Chichester being the first to successfully brave the Great Capes in 1966 and Willie de Roos, the first to thread the needle of the Northwest Passage in 1977. Though the accomplishment of either remains a significant undertaking for the amateur sailor, combining the two into a single attempt had apparently escaped the notice of more rational souls until I happened upon it as the answer to a challenge from my wife.

That challenge: *"If you are going to go off on another cruise, at least make it a big one."* I had been dreaming of the south since reading Knox-Johnson and Moitessier and of the north since Tillman. Having just singlehanded the

Pacific in the two years previous, I was eager for more and a solo circumnavigation of both the American and Antarctica continents in a single season was simply the biggest thing I could think of at the time.

Early Preparations

The idea struck in 2012. In 2013, I began to scope the requirements, to define the distances, the optimal timings, and the characteristics of the appropriate vessel.

One difficulty, however, did not resolve with research—the Northwest Passage. From reading alone, I simply could not grok how to negotiate the narrow, poorly charted channels and the pack ice that clogged them. So, I took the opportunity in 2014 to crew an Arctic attempt with Les and Ali Parsons on their steel sloop, *Arctic Tern*. Due to ice concentrations in the archipelago that year, only seven boats of thirty were able to complete the course, and all seven were made of metal.

Using what I knew from earlier passages and what I learned in the north that year, I began looking in 2015 for a metal boat for the Figure 8 Voyage. In 2016, she was found in a yard in Homer, Alaska; purchased, renamed *Moli* (referred to throughout as *Mo*), and singlehanded back to San Francisco via stops in Washington and Hawaii.

(Photo Credit: Kim Kirsch)

A Failed Attempt

LEG: San Francisco to San Francisco ★ DATES: October 28, 2017 to July 9, 2018 ★ DAYS: 253 ★ DAYS AT SEA: 205 ★ NAUTICAL MILES: 26,453

Preparations for the Figure 8 Voyage had begun in 2013, but they kicked into high gear when *Mo* and I returned to San Francisco from the Pacific shakedown cruise of 2016. Here, the first order of business was to pull the mast and put *Mo* under a tent at the KKMI boatyard so that I could strip and paint the decks throughout the winter months.

Mo **under** her winter tent that allowed me to pursue a deck paint job during the wet months.

But that was just the start. *Mo* received entirely new standing and running rigging at KKMI and then new sails from the Hood shop in Sausalito; my friends at Scanmar International pulled and rebuilt *Mo's* Monitor windvane; electronics were updated; solar panels were augmented with a hydrogenator hung from the transom; fuel and water tanks were emptied and cleaned, the rudder was dropped and inspected; the shaft and propeller remade. Only then, late summer 2017, was *Mo* ready to receive the full year's worth of stores that had been stockpiling at the house.

Last-minute delays pushed an October 1st departure to later and later in the month, and it wasn't until the foggy morning of October 28 that *Mo* and I finally cast off from Horseshoe Cove and sailed out under the

Ross and Ichiro of Scanmar International are carefully installing *Mo's* rebuilt Monitor windvane.

Golden Gate Bridge. A small flotilla followed as far as Point Bonita. Then we were on our own. The Figure 8 had finally begun.

I quickly fell into the rhythm of being at sea, the daily sail changes, course adjustments, chores and short sleeps, and the longer-term changes felt as we passed down the Pacific and from northwesterlies to trade winds to doldrums and back to trades. Soon *Mo* and I were approaching southern high latitudes, where our adventure true was to commence.

By December 16, our 49th day at sea, we had achieved 52 degrees south and were shaping a final course for Cape Horn when we were overtaken by our first southern gale and the first big blow *Mo* and I had experienced together. At the height of it, winds topped 50 knots and were gusting 70, in the final phase and as seas built up tremendously, *Mo* was knocked well over to starboard. I was thrown against the pilothouse windows as they turned green, and a small amount of water squirted in through the companionway hatch. *Mo* came immediately upright, but I soon discovered that some of the invading seawater had made

Hauling *Mo* at KKMI for new prop and propshaft and new bottom paint.

Bending on *Mo's* new HOOD mainsail.

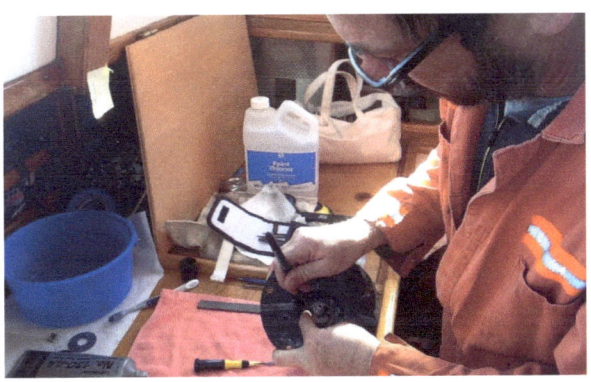

Rebuilding *Mo's* winches.

In April of 2017, *Mo* and I took a break from work and both attended the local boat show. Tony Gooch was our guest and helped explain the Figure 8 to the many attendees.

Over the winter, the living room slowly filled with the year's worth of stores I wanted aboard by departure day.

Beginning to load stores aboard *Mo*. *(Photo Credit: Joe Rosato Jr.)*

Departure. October 28, 2017. A small flotilla and media boat follow *Mo* as far as Point Bonita. *(Photo Credit: Heather Richard.)*

***Mo* and I** soon fall into the rhythm of being at sea--including daily tricks with the dish brush.

Chores on deck are many but seem always to include some variant of cranking in a line, coiling it or dealing with its chafe.

A few days below the line, and well before the southeast trades kick in, *Mo* and I are treated to a full night of lightning.

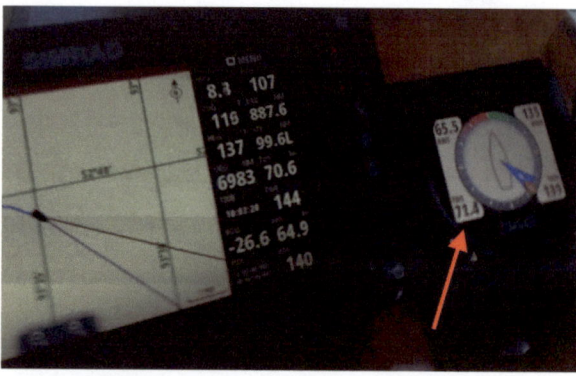

During our first gale in the Roaring Forties, winds, as recorded on the anemometer, blew a steady fifty knots and gusted to seventy.

Just days from Cape Horn and in the latter phase of this low, a large sea put *Mo* well over and a small amount of seawater made its way into the pilothouse.

During the grueling week of hand steering required to make for safety, I took no photos, until here we are raising the coast of Chile.

Now we are within the ever-straight Beagle Channel and are motoring for safety. A blow from offshore has left a dusting of snow on the mountains. It's Christmas Day.

Anchor down, Caletta Olla. In the dark of night, I had mistaken the entrance to this cove and had run aground on a lee beach during a blizzard of sleet.

Within a few days, *Mo* is tucked-in safely against the Club AFASyN jetty in Ushuaia.

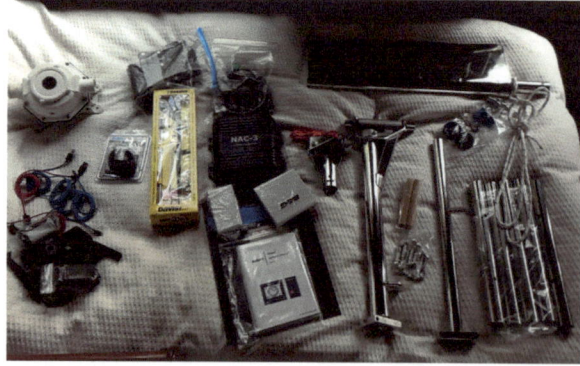

When my wife, Joanna, arrives, her suitcase holds a great number of treasures.

Ragged cloud over the Argentinian Navy Pier just south of Ushuaia.

its way into the port-side electronics cabinet, shorting out the autopilot computer.

Though disappointing, this had no immediate consequences, as *Monte* (the new name for my ablest crewmember, the windvane) did all the steering when *Mo* was under sail. However, four days later, a non-serviceable part on *Monte's* water paddle failed. The moment I fished the broken piece from the sea, I knew we were in dire straits. Suddenly, at 56 degrees south and with Cape Horn 400 miles due east, I had no way to automatically steer the boat. Continuing on with the

Figure 8 was impossible; now we were in survival mode.

For five days, I hand steered in shifts as long as I was able. Typical Southern Ocean winds and seas meant the pressures on *Mo's* short tiller were tremendous, often taking me to the edge of my physical capacity. Six-hour tricks at the tiller chilled me right through, even though I was working hard and wearing triple layers. Breaks below to warm up and take on more calories often consisted of three cans of beans and pasta heated to boiling and then eaten as quickly as possible. After twelve

to eighteen hours of progress, I'd let *Mo* lie ahull at night, and in this manner we made our slow approach to Chile's Bahia Cook.

We sat out Christmas Eve on the Jordan Series Drogue while a brutal northerly blew through, and a day later were entering the great bay, then the Beagle Channel, and finally Caletta Olla, a perfectly round cove where I was directed by my friend, Tony Gooch, as it was one of the few places in the Chile Channels where a small sailboat could ride safely at single anchor.

Above: **By January 11,** *Mo* is ready for sea, and we departed Ushuaia for the great Southern Ocean.

Below: **Lofting the genoa poles** in a seaway always takes a goodly measure of concentration and coordination.

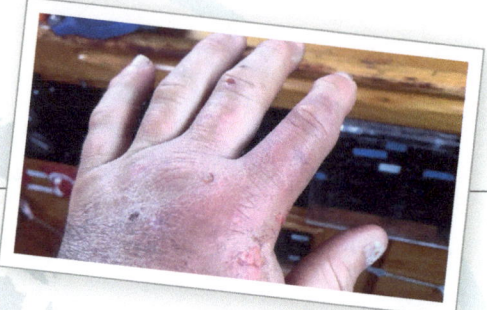

My left hand received a bit of a sprain when it got fouled in the drogue that was feeding over the side. I was lucky it hadn't been worse, but the swelling hung around for several days.

On December 28, our 58th day at sea, *Mo* and I arrived in Ushuaia, Argentina for repairs. I was met at the dock by Roxanna Diaz, the local Port Captain for the Ocean Cruising Club, who kindly ferried me to the several offices whose stamp was required on my passport, directly after which she pointed the way to the yacht club's hot showers. Soon after, my wife, Joanna, arrived with a suitcase full of spare parts, and I immediately went to work on getting *Mo* ship-shape. *Mo* and I departed Ushuaia to the east on January 11, 2018. The Figure 8 Voyage had resumed.

By Valentine's Day, we had passed under Cape Good Hope, were well out into the Indian Ocean, and were pressing northeast toward the Crozet Islands, attempting to get above a large low that had been tracking to our position for several days. On February 16 and at 46.42 degrees south, *Mo* and I passed close enough to Cochon and Pinguino Islands to see them as darker gray smudges on the gray horizon. And then the low descended.

On the morning of February 17, winds were well over thirty knots from the northwest; by evening they were well over forty. What was remarkable, however, were the seas, which were steep and breaking heavily. Often the solid wall of white water extended for several hundred feet. By nightfall, we were running under storm jib alone, and I struggled in the rain and absolute dark to find a position that would allow *Mo* to ride comfortably. We were thrown down repeatedly. At sunrise, the wind had gone into the west, and I gybed around to take the larger, new set of seas more directly astern. I was wedged into the pilothouse with a cup of coffee when *Mo* was picked up by a particularly large sea, spun to port, and thrown bodily over into the trough.

I remember the sensation of the fall, the softness of the landing; I remember water gushing into the pilothouse in a thick, green stream; now I could hear the gale loudly; I could see water clearly through a hole in the portside. And only then did I realize that the window over the electronics bay had been shattered by the sea.

Suddenly and again, *Mo* and I were in survival mode. Unsure what to do first, I pumped the bilges dry while I thought through a plan. Clearly, I would not be able to make *Mo* safe under sail in these seas, so the first essential thing was to deploy the Jordan Series Drogue. Once the boat was stopped, I went below

to close the gaping hole in the pilothouse. My detailed preparations, I knew, had not included storm windows, but I soon found two bunk boards from the forecastle that bolted easily in place. The gaps left by their imperfect fit were filled with silicon.

Water and glass were everywhere below, and I had just begun the long job of clean-up when I noticed a change in boat motion. A glance out the window showed we were lying

During the February 18 gale, *Mo* is thrown to the bottom of a sea and one of her port-side windows is shattered. Here that window has been patched up with two bunk-boards from the forecastle. Note the shattered glass strewn about the table top.

Cutting away the bent aluminum rail and smashed solar panel, the effect of one of the knockdowns in the Indian Ocean gale.

The front of an intense low approaching just as *Mo* and I are dipping behind Tasmania's South East Cape.

March 18. Constitution Dock, Hobart, Tasmania. Tired, but relieved. (Note boarded up window).

Hobart under threatening skies.

This is Captian John Solomon aboard his *Sole Mio*. Solomon was the first to welcome *Mo* and her skipper to Hobart and was a great resource.

A sunny day in Hobart as seen through *Mo's* broken window.

Sunday afternoon Dragon races on the River Derwent. Darryl Ridgeway *(gray foulies)* came daily to *Mo's* aid during her stay. *(Photo Credit: John Solomon)*

On a mooring at Barnes Bay the day before departing Hobart for San Francisco.

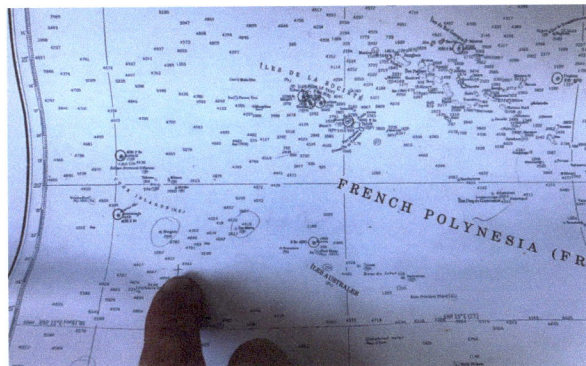

From Hobart, *Mo* and I pass under New Zealand and then through the Cook Islands on our way home.

dangerously ahull. On deck, I tugged on the drogue bridle and found it pulled in easily. The line had parted at the eye splice—the drogue was gone. Quickly, I put *Mo* before the wind and we rode the remainder of the blow under bare poles without further mishap.

But the damage had been done, and it was extensive. Directly under the broken window was *Mo's* navigation station, which had been entirely inundated with water during that final knockdown. Now dead were the single sideband radio, the VHF radio, barometer and two of three satellite communications devices. Knockdowns during the night had bent an aft rail in and over the winches, shattering one of the solar panels. And enough water had pressed in through the pilothouse window to fill the bilge up to the engine; it had also flowed into the fuel tanks through the vents such that when I cranked the engine later, seawater flooded the injectors. Worst of all, the blow had taken our chief safety device, the drogue.

Again, *Mo* and I would have to put into port for repairs, and this time the delay would mean the end of the Figure 8 Voyage. Now we would be too late in the year for a safe, second approach to Cape Horn, and even our timely arrival to the Arctic would be in jeopardy. During the month of sailing required to make Hobart, Tasmania, I contemplated what to do.

On March 18, our 124th day out of San Francisco, *Mo* and I were greeted at the Royal Yacht Club of Tasmania by Ocean Cruising Club Port Captain John Solomon, and within moments, I had been introduced to a great number of people who could help get *Mo* back on her feet. Tony Gooch had made these arrangements for us well in advance of my arrival, and waiting there was a new drogue in addition to the friendly faces.

One club member, Daryll Ridgeway, became *Mo's* sponsor for the duration of our stay, arranging the welding of *Mo's* rail, the acquisition of new glass for the window and endless rides into town for supplies. A week later, Joanna also arrived, again with a suitcase full of spare parts from the States.

By late April, *Mo* was ship shape and ready for sea, but where would she be headed? Homeward. Back to San Francisco to start the Figure 8 all over again.

On April 23, *Mo* and I departed Hobart to the east. We passed under New Zealand on April 30, to the west of the Cook Islands on May 22,

and crossed the line on the first of June. After a brief stop in Hawaii, *Mo* and I headed first north and then east and sighted the Golden Gate Bridge on July 9, 2018. We had sailed over 26,000 miles in the 253 days since our departure. We had failed to complete the Figure 8 Voyage, but we had circumnavigated the globe, and we were home.

Mo **sails under the Golden Gate Bridge** on July 9, 2018 after 190 days since departure. We have circumnavigated in that time but had failed to complete the Figure 8 Voyage. *(Photo Credit, top: Joanna Bloor, right, Eric Moe.)*

A Second Chance

LEG: San Francisco to Cape Horn ★ DATES: October 4 to November 29, 2018 ★ DAYS: 56
NAUTICAL MILES: 7,471 ★ AVERAGE MILES PER DAY: 133 ★ DAYS ON WHICH WINDS ATTAINED GALE FORCE: 6
DAYS ON WHICH WERE BECALMED: 5 ★ ON DECK TEMPERATURE RANGE: 46°- 89°F

September 30, 2018, departure day for the second attempt at the Figure 8 Voyage, dawned clear. No fog hung over the Golden Gate Bridge; the water-top in Horseshoe Cove lay still and glassy.

That morning I felt strangely relaxed. On departure day the year before, I had been consumed with an uneasiness driven by ignorance. Then I didn't know what I'd be up against in the raging Southern Ocean. Now I knew. *Mo* and I had faced the worst of it and lost, but we had survived.

The plan to sail home from Australia for a second try that same year had left a scant three months for preparations—for provisioning, repairs, an audit of the spares list and more study of the route. But I felt ready. By this point, *Mo* could not be made any stronger, and amazingly, I was still eager for the challenge ahead.

I hugged friends on the quay. *Mo* and I motored out surrounded by another small flotilla. Again, Jo drove to Point Bonita for a final phone call, and this time I could see her. We waved and waved.

Then, to my joy, *Mo* picked up a small wind from the northwest. I unfurled the big genoa and we slid slowly out on the tide. By afternoon we had nearly sunk the land, but here, as the forecast had foretold, the wind died entirely, and it did not return. Faced with the prospect of bobbing in the shipping channel for three days, I quietly switched on the engine and motored the few miles north along the coast to Drakes Bay, where we anchored while the dead remains of a Pacific hurricane moved slowly to the north.

By October 4, a northwesterly wind had filled in again. I weighed anchor in the early morning and soon we were slipping past the Farallon Islands and out to sea. I knew this would be our last view of land until we raised Cape Horn. The wind increased. Soon the islands were far behind. What Jo and I had dubbed the Figure 8 Voyage 2.0 had begun.

Left: **September 30,** 2018. *Mo* is heading for the Golden Gate Bridge on her second Figure 8 attempt. *(Photo Credit: Tim Henry)*

Top: **Feeling relaxed**, I wave to friends as we depart. *(Photo Credit: Tim Henry)*

Above: **October 4,** 2018. Passing under the Farallon Islands out to sea.

Facing Page: **Headed south.** The coastal marine layer has cleared, but long sleeves, the cottony cumulus and an easy sea mean we've not yet made the NE trades winds.

Top and bottom left: **Day 7.** First of many messages in a bottle. This one is inscribed, "*Please tell my wife, Joanna, that I love her and to be sure to clean the leaves off the roof before it rains.*"

Above: **Not brilliant.** I'm splicing an eye in the new topnlift, but I forgot to insert the snap shackle before finishing the loop.

One of the pleasures of being
at sea is the ready access the sailor
has to expansive views, of waves,
of clouds, and sunsets over
the horizon.

Left: **In the tropical latitudes,** boobies often approached *Mo* in search of an easy roost. This bird I named Scraggle because he insisted on using the slippery solar panel as a perch, which required he claw and scratch to stay put. He remained with us for two days.

Above: **Day 20.** Crossing the equator and becoming a Shellback with a bottle of sparkling wine.

Facing page: **The complex cloud** of unsettled weather as we push further south.

Above left: **Day 24.** We have achieved 29S, and on this day, amazingly, we spy our first albatross, a sure sign that we are making an approach to southern high latitudes.

Above center: **There's always** something in need of repair. Here one of the mainsail cars on the mast track has lost its bearings and must be replaced.

Above: ***Mo's* albatross burgee,** the gift of Darryl Ridgeway, my friend from Hobart, is beginning to show signs of the miles, though it has only been at the crosstrees since the previous May.

Facing Page: **Now wind and sea** are picking up. *Mo* is making fast time.

Above and right: **Day 49**. *Mo* has achieved 50S, and here we are overtaken by our first serious blow, four straight days of Force 8 winds from the northwest. By the second day, the seas are long trains of massive breakers. I spent my watches in the pilot house in awe of the vast amounts of energy in motion.

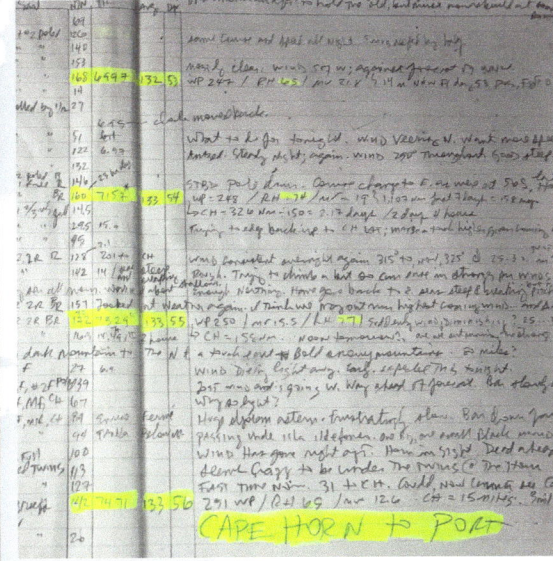

Above right: **Mo's log,** updated every two hours with position, course and speed notes the accomplishment in bold, *"Cape Horn to Port."*

Facing page: **Day 56.** At last the goal, Cape Horn, rises slowly, majestically from the sea. We are fortunate that now the wind has eased, and though the day remains drizzly, *Mo* and I are able to slide in below the great rock and feast our eyes upon this most historic of promontories. How easily this compensates for the now-forgotten disappointments of the first attempt.

Over the Bounding Main

LEG: Cape Horn to Cape Horn ★ DATES: November 30, 2018 to March 20, 2019 ★ DAYS: 110
NAUTICAL MILES: 15,512 ★ AVERAGE MILES PER DAY: 140 ★ DAYS ON WHICH WINDS ATTAINED GALE FORCE: 16
DAYS ON WHICH WERE BECALMED: 6 ★ ON DECK TEMPERATURE RANGE: 44° - 64°F

I wrote in the log on November 30, …not just to round the Great Cape, satisfaction plenty, nor even to have it hove into view from afar, but to run up to within a mile such that I could see the slabs of black rock, the olive-green mosses, the lighthouse. To hear the massive rollers booming from the cliff after their run around the globe; to shudder at the thought of approaching on a dirty night, such is Cape Horn.

"All past now. Under cover of cloud, we ran in utter darkness toward Isla de los Estatos while I slept six hours and was only up once. In the gloom of morning, I could see the island in silhouette, and on we run…"

Though this was a milestone for the Figure 8 Voyage, any pleasure I felt was mixed with the knowledge that the Horn was not an end but the beginning of our true challenge. Now we were embedded in the wild Southern Ocean, and to be successful, here we would remain until we passed below the Horn again. To do that would mean sailing twice as far as we had already come, three months and more in the Roaring Forties. Did I have the will, the stamina, to withstand what I knew the south could deliver? Did *Mo* have the strength to survive so long below 45 degrees south? I did not know, but it was what we were here to find out.

Within a week, we are overtaken by a large low-pressure system with winds of 45 knots accompanied by a breathtaking sea. While I am resting below in the half-light of morning, *Mo* is pooped. The boat goes hard over; water slams against the pilothouse and sprays into the cabin through a gap in the companionway hatch. On deck, I see the Monitor airvane has been ripped from its socket. Inexplicably, it is not lost but wedged between the rail and cleats of the back deck. *Mo* suffers no other damage. But this is our welcome to the Southern Ocean.

Facing page: **Our first gale after departing Cape Horn** brought breathtaking seas. *Mo* is pooped but suffers no serious damage. After it passes, I take the opportunity to dry clothes in the cockpit.

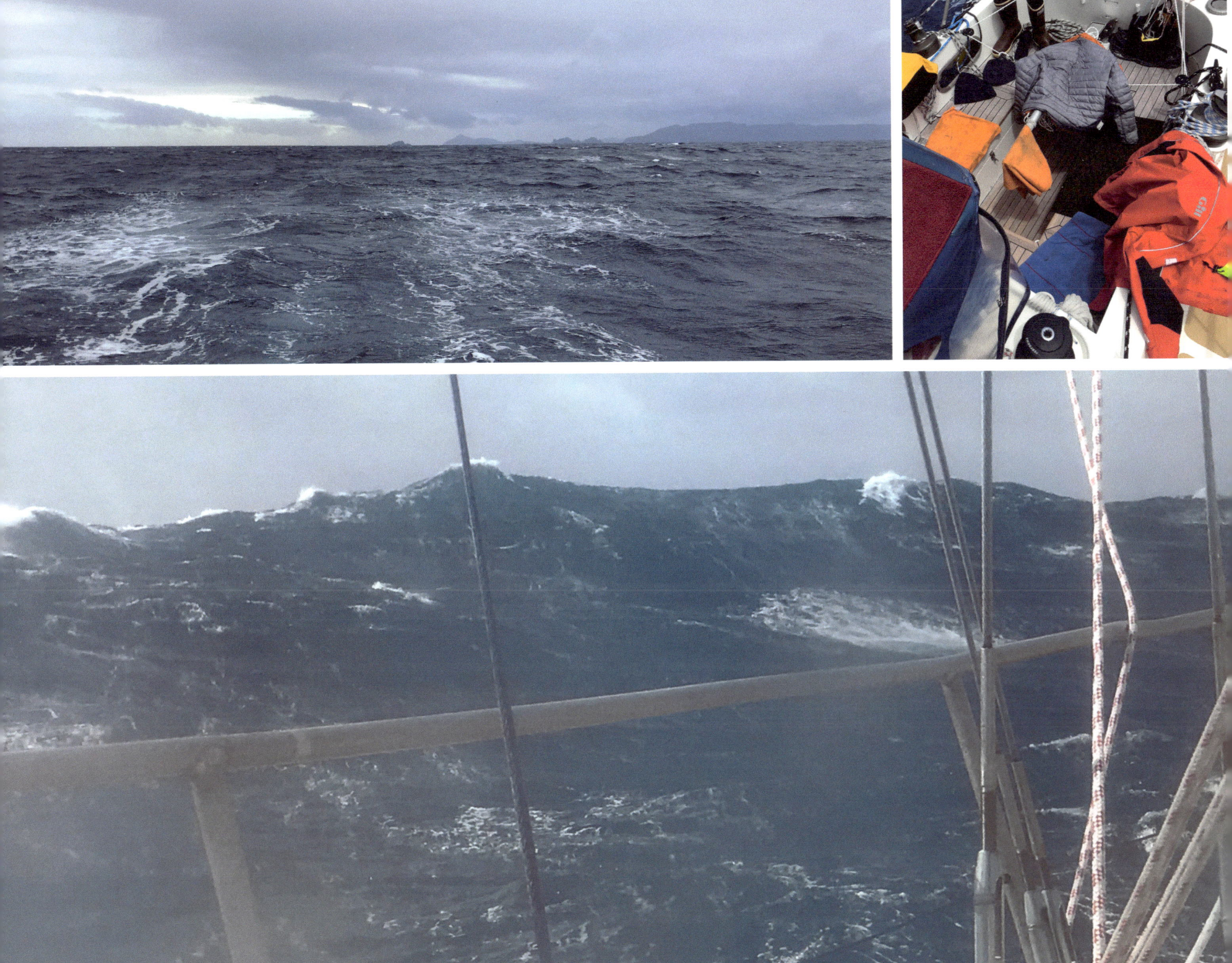

Top: **Large seas are the norm** in the south, and watching them from the pilothouse becomes a favorite pastime. Here, and even on a cloudy day, the camera has caught a flash of turquoise through the crest of an otherwise sapphire sea.

Inset: **How to protect hardworking hands** is a continual challenge. Full gloves or mittens would guard against the cold, but the fingers must be able to function. For me, the best solution was old technology-- woolen, fingerless gloves.

Facing Page, top left: **Route planning** with dividers based on twice-daily weather forecasts; *middle:* **One sea over the stern** tore a flap off the companionway covers, here being mended by hand; *right:* **When it's cold and rough,** keeping clean takes discipline. A head and beard wash once a week was the best I could muster.

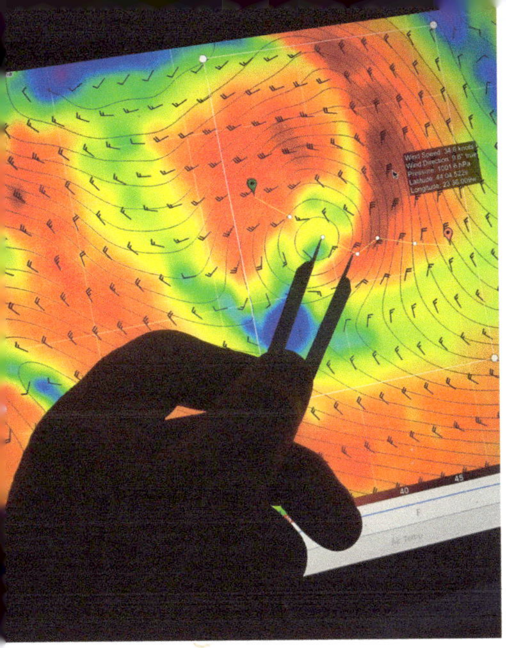
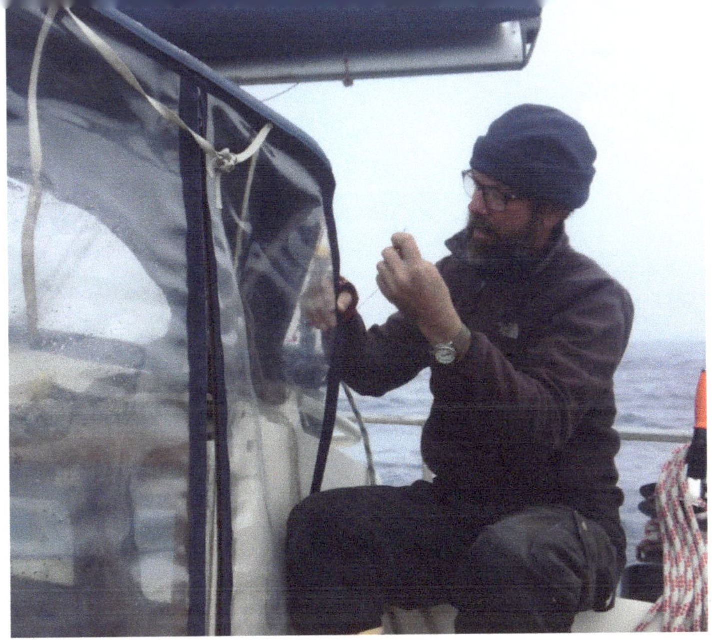
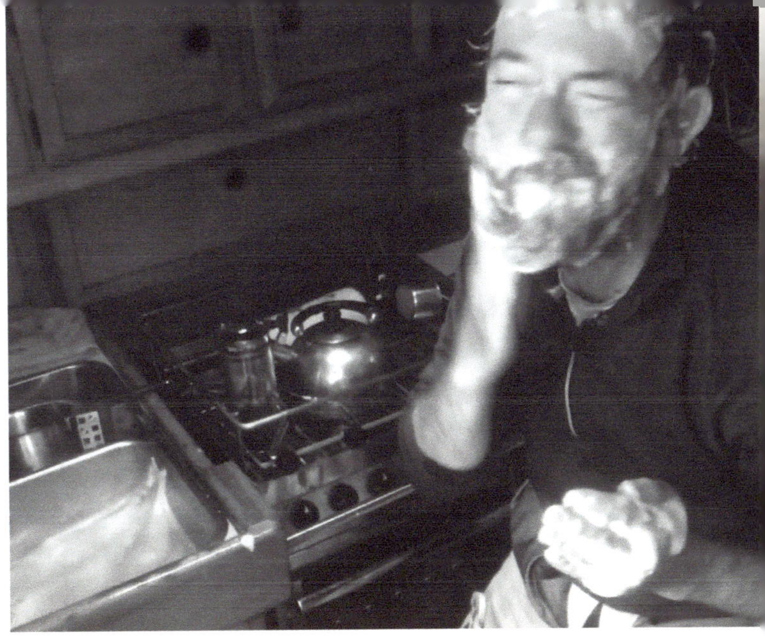
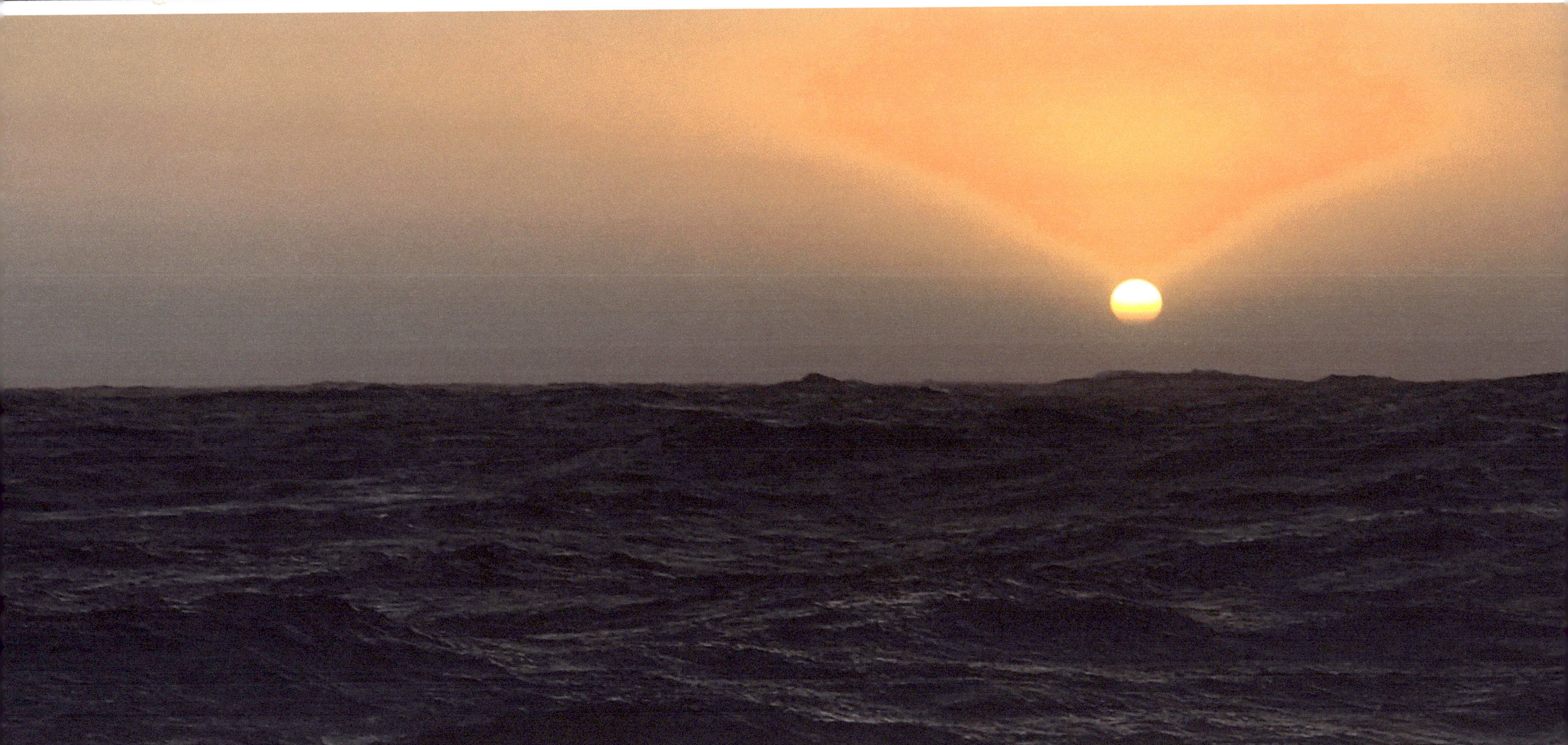

Top: **Mo comes to the end** of a surfing run in big following seas; *bottom left:* **Day 80.** It's December 23 and today we are crossing the prime meridian; time for a whiteboard picture; *bottom right:* **Day 83.** It's Christmas. Upon departure, Jo had given me a large box from the family, which I kept stowed in the forepeak until the appointed time. The box held gifts and cards of encouragement, many of which I taped to the Christmas Tree--which is to say, the mast. Buried deep was even a box of chocolate. What thoughtfulness.

Facing Page: **Not every day is a gale.** Here *Mo* has a bone in her teeth on a wind from the south.

Above: **Chafe,** the bane of the sailor. Here I am changing out the windward jib sheet after a long run on the poles. *Inset:* The pink, high-tech downhaul line on the hydrogenerator lasts only a few thousand miles before chafing through.

Facing page, left: **Every day** of good weather must be used to accomplish chores on deck. Here I'm redoing a soft-tie for the genoa pole lines; *middle:* **Hands are often wet** and swollen, especially if they spend hours in woolen gloves; *right:* **A Skua** examines *Mo* from height; *bottom:* **Relaxing under the protection** of the dodger as *Mo* makes way to the east.

Facing page: **Birds are one's all-weather companions** in the south. Here Prions play in the wind eddies created by a breaking sea.

Above, left: **An immature Wandering Albatross** wanders by; *center:* Chocolate brown **White-Chinned Petrels** often played in *Mo's* wake searching for food; *right:* **Cape Petrels,** also known as Pintados, were a favorite because of their markings and because they would swoop in close to the boat.

Above: **Working the mainsail** on a lighter wind day.

Inset: **Donning gloves is not always convenient** when one has to make the deck in a hurry, and if the issue takes time to resolve, hands can turn red from the cold and then go numb before one has a chance to get below.

Facing page, top left: **Baking bread** had the advantage of providing heat to an otherwise unheated cabin. Warm bread, canned butter, home-made jam--a bit of heaven.

Facing page, middle, right and bottom: **On average,** *Mo* was overtaken by a low a week as she made her way around Antarctica. These systems were announced by a falling barometer, whose readings I would circle in the log until the pressure began to rise again. Towering seas were always the accompaniment.

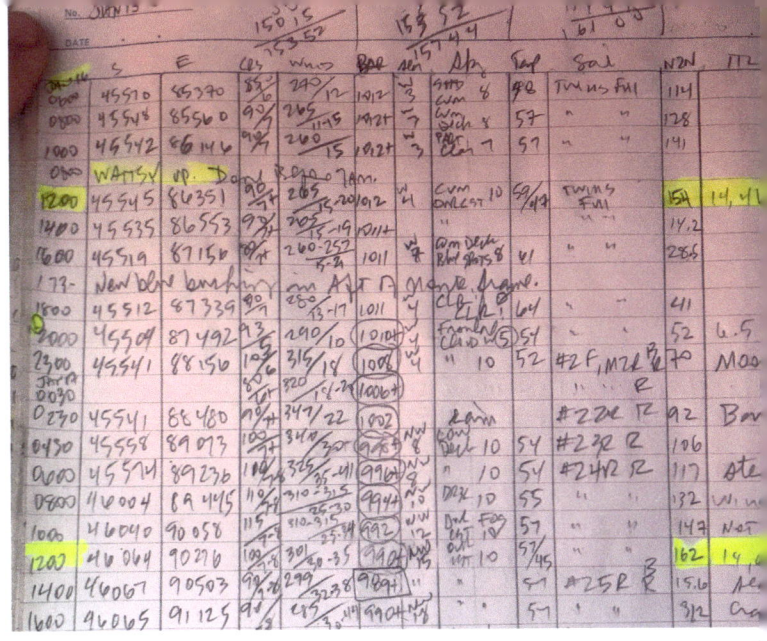

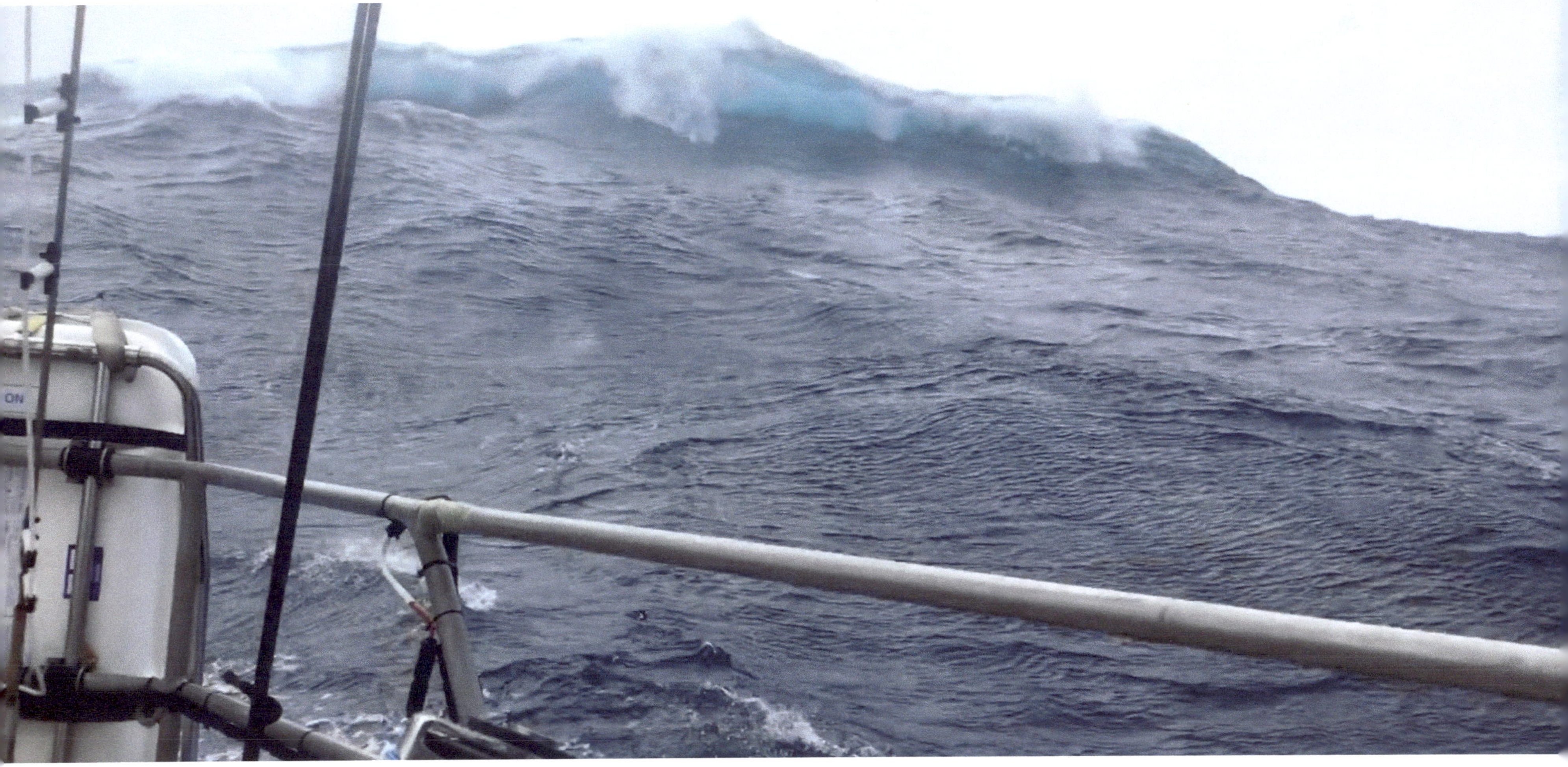

Top left: **Typically I cook enough dinner** for two meals, which requires I cook only every other night. But in the south, one is working hard, and extra calories are needed for warmth. So, frequently I would cook a triple portion and then eat all of it in one sitting.

Bottom left: **Drying boots** in the relative warmth under the dodger.

Top right: **Bit by bit,** *Mo's* albatross burgee is wearing away in the constant high winds.

Bottom right and opposite: **Day 116.** Another intense low, as seen on the weather chart, passes to the south as we slide under Australia. Its aftermath brings great green rollers.

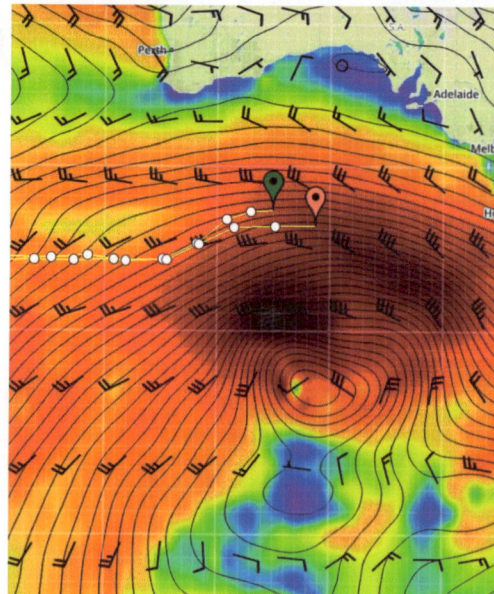

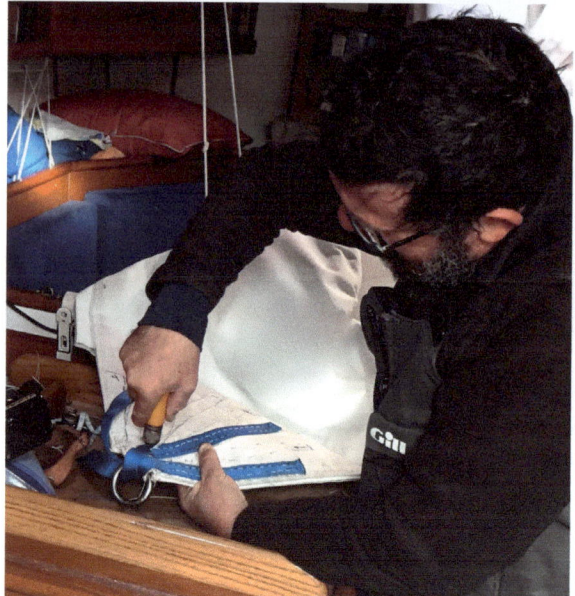

Above: **Day 124.** I discover the clew webbing on the working jib has nearly worn through. The sail was new when *Mo* departed San Francisco for the first attempt, but by now it has nearly 40,000 miles to its credit and has been in constant use since its first lofting. I quickly swap it for the spare, pull it below and stitch on new webbing. The operation takes several days, and in the process, I break my entire stock of awl needles.

Above left: **Sleeping** in *Mo's* main cabin, safely tucked behind a lee cloth.

Facing page, top: **Repairing** the genoa pole while it's in use.

Facing page, bottom: **I regularly caught rainwater** in the south via fittings on the mainsail cover and manually transferred that catch to the keel tanks. When, much later, we arrived in Halifax, we still had half our water onboard.

The handwritten sign in the photo reads:

CAPE HORN²

- ONE FULL LOOP BELOW CAPES
- INCLUDING TWO ROUNDINGS OF CAPE HORN ✓ DONE!
- NON-STOP / SOLO

SOUTH AMERICA

CAPE HORN

CAPE HORN TO CAPE HORN

→ 1ST PASS 11/29/18
→ 2ND PASS 3/20/19

110 DAYS
15,343 MILES
JUST MŌ & RANDALL

EVER DONE BEFORE?

NZ

Above and facing page: **Day 167.** Our last blow comes a day before the Horn. I have been planning to remain south of Diego Ramirez but can't resist a final sighting. I change course for the northeast and *Mo* races while I watch from under the dodger. Then the rock hoves into view. Now winds are 30 knots, but skies are clear as *Mo* passes beneath Cape Horn for the second time. Our full loop of the south has taken 110 days.

The Long, Slow Climb

LEG: Cape Horn to Halifax ★ DATES: March 20 to May 31, 2019 ★ DAYS: 72 ★ NAUTICAL MILES: 8,265
AVERAGE MILES PER DAY: 115 ★ DAYS ON WHICH WINDS ATTAINED GALE FORCE: 2
DAYS ON WHICH WERE BECALMED: 8 ★ ON DECK TEMPERATURE RANGE: 46° - 91°F

Mo and I rounded Cape Horn for the second time on March 20, and by the first of April had cleared the Roaring Forties heading north on a beat. Northing, what a novelty! We had spent over three months focused only on easting. Even now it was a rough ride, but soon winds would soften and warm. I smiled at the prospect of smooth sailing with trade winds below and above the equator. Here I could relax and take up chores and repairs the extreme south has not allowed.

And the turn brought with it a sense of anticipation. For me, the Atlantic was new territory and would feature different weather patterns, different bird life, and a different history. Moreover, we were, for the first time, on our approach to the Arctic. The south had required complete attention, but now I could begin to contemplate the challenges awaiting us there.

In fact, the long run back to the line was bedeviled by light and contrary winds, and in the doldrums, Mo encountered days and days of oppressive calms and entrapping islands of Sargasso weed. Above the line, the trade winds failed to develop much strength. As we made our slow way past the Caribbean and then Bermuda, I watched with frustration as our daily averages declined.

Thus, I met with some joy the approach of a strong low from the mainland. For two days we rode north on its gale-force southwest winds, and for another two, Mo held her position by riding the drogue. Seas towered, due in large part to our having entered the strong northeasterly current of the Gulf Stream.

On the final leg, winds again became fitful and brought with them a thick fog that persisted even as we made the port of Halifax, Nova Scotia. Out of the murk came a green buoy and then the outer harbor lighthouse. And then, and for the first time in months, a coastline covered in trees. Here Mo found safe haven after 237 days at sea and 31,589 miles since her departure from San Francisco.

Above and right: **Weather is unsettled** until well above the Falkland Islands. *Above:* Routine maintenance on the windvane; *Right:* Close hauled to the north and repairing a parted main topnlift.

Above and left: **Day 190.** It's mid-April. *Mo* and I have entered the luxury of the Atlantic's southeast trades. Now I can nap in the cockpit in short sleeves and do laundry in the sunshine. Flying fish are regularly found in the scuppers. It's a grand life, but shortlived. Winds are light this year. Soon the sails are gasping for air.

Above and right: **As we approach the Doldrums,** days alternate. Some are low and drenching while others are open and bring a blistering sun. We pass slowly through rafts of Sargasso weed, where I fear *Mo* may be held captive for a ransom unknown. And then we enter the doldrums proper. What wind there was evaporates; the sky is heavy with squalls.

Left: **Day 215.** By middle May, we have nearly achieved 20N. Winds are steady but continue light, and even flying the spinnaker can't keep our average mileage from dropping. It's a slow run. No matter; life at sea has many pleasures, and one of them is maintaining a log of celestial navigation.

Above and left: **Day 232.** Now we are close to our goal, but the north Atlantic has another lesson yet to teach. On May 25, a low drops in and brings with it northeasterlies of 45 knots. I have misjudged our position in the Gulf Stream for my deployment of the drogue, and soon the seas are dangerously steep and breaking. At one point, a sea fouls the drogue bridle in the windvane, inflicting damage, but nothing that stops us from carrying on.

Left: **May 31, 2019.** A deep fog has enveloped us for days, and winds have been light. But in the middle afternoon, we finally raise the outer-harbor lighthouse of Halifax, Nova Scotia. Here *Mo* comes to rest after 31,589 miles and 237 days from San Francisco.

The Northwest Passage

LEG: Halifax to San Francisco ★ DATES: July 2 to October 19, 2019 ★ DAYS: 99 ★ NAUTICAL MILES: 7,796
DAYS ON WHICH WINDS ATTAINED GALE FORCE: 3 ★ DAYS ON WHICH BECALMED: Above 50N, most days were calm
ICEBERGS: Most frequent between Disko Bay and Sondre Upernavik, Greenland ★ PACK ICE: Most concentrated
between the top of Peel Sound and Victoria Strait ★ ON DECK TEMPERATURE RANGE: 34°- 65°F

After so many days at sea, *Mo* and I enjoyed a brief rest in Halifax and the hospitality of many new friends at the Nova Scotia Royal Yacht Squadron. While here, I also took the opportunity to reprovision and to recommission equipment—like the cabin's diesel heater and the anchor windlass—that had gone unused during the long ocean passage but that would now be vital to our survival.

Another key component to our success in the north, *Mo's* diminutive red engine, was thoroughly inspected and both the starter motor and the alternator were replaced with new from the spares in the forepeak.

The challenges in the Arctic would be extreme, I knew, but they would also be extremely different from what *Mo* and I had experienced in the Southern Ocean. Endless expanses of consistently high winds and seas would be replaced with a maze of shallow, poorly charted inland waterways, light, erratic winds and—most importantly—the constant threat of pack ice. Now I would be relying on pilotage skills and the engine to make way.

Moreover, this passage would be a race against time. Summer in the high north is but a brief interlude between long, dark winters. In a typical year, a yacht like *Mo* has approximately two months to make the roughly 5,000 nautical miles from the Arctic circle on one side of the passage to the Arctic circle on the other. The area is remote; the chances of being stopped by ice are high; one is on his own and must be prepared for anything.

By July 2, 2019, preparations were complete. *Mo* and I departed Halifax for happy but brief stops in St. John's, Newfoundland and the villages of the west coast of Greenland before crossing the Arctic Circle on July 26, where we entered the Northwest Passage proper.

Above: **June 7, 2019.** *Mo* being prepared for new bottom paint in the weighs at the Nova Scotia Yacht Squadron at Halifax.

Centre left: **Taking on provision for the Arctic.** Though I expected to be home before winter, I carried enough stores for many months of Arctic uncertainty.

Top left and previous: **In typical summer Arctic calms,** we would be relying on the engine, so "Big Red" received numerous inspections and upgrades, which gave me greasy hands for days.

Bottom left: **Rebuilding** the windvane on the luxuriously level surface of a marina dock.

Above: **On July 3,** *Mo* and I departed Halifax bound for St. John's, Newfoundland and the Arctic. *(Photo Credit: Sebastiaan Ambtman)*

Above: **The passage to Greenland** delivered calms complicated by fog and cold rain, and it wasn't until we neared the capital city of Nuuk that the sky cleared to reveal the high coastal ranges below the icecap.

Bottom, left: **Mo passes** a bright red Royal Arctic Line resupply ship, a common sight in Greenland waters; *right, Mo* is rafted to a workboat in Nuuk's busy inner harbor.

Above: **Nuuk's old town center** guarded by a bronze statue of founder, Hanz Egede.

Left: **Dwarf Fireweed,** the Greenland national flower, decorates the granite hills above the harbor.

Left: **By July 26,** *Mo* and I had crossed the Arctic circle at 66.30N, but we still had a great deal of northing yet to make.

Right: **An old red barn** and an old green fishing boat are picturesquely positioned above Sisimiut harbor.

Bottom: **Mo** **on a reach** in an unusually brisk Arctic wind and accompanied by icebergs. *(Photo Credit: Vincent Moeyersoms)*

Above, right and facing page: **When *Mo* and I crossed the Arctic Circle** and made our approach to Disko Bay, the ice concentration increased dramatically. Here the fjords are stacked with glaciers that, in the summer, calve icebergs by the score into Disko and the Vaigut. Many ground out on the shoals near shore, but those bergs that escaped the sound are destined to drift far out to sea.

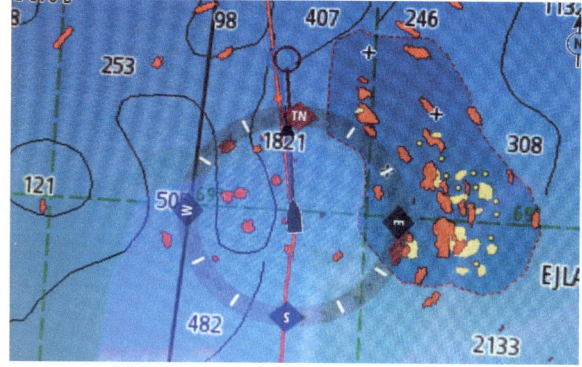

Right: **On August 9, day 313** of the Figure 8 Voyage, *Mo* and I anchored off Pond Inlet below the dramatic ranges of Bylot Island, our first stop in the Canadian Arctic. *(Photo Credit: Vincent Moeyersoms)*

Facing page: **Mo anchored in entirely enclosed Hatt Trick Harbor** at the base of Navy Board Inlet, one of the most perfect, all-weather coves I have ever discovered.

Above right: **Westward view from the hills surrounding Tay Bay** off the north arm of Navy Board Inlet. Note the shotgun, which I carried for protection against Polar Bears.

Above left: **Reindeer antlers** in the hills and an empty, abandoned fuel drum on the beach were among the finds in Tay Bay.

Facing page: **The remarkable tabletop mountains** and fluted cliffs of south Devon Island off Lancaster Sound. The aridity and desert-like features of the Arctic are initially surprising to one who expects nothing but expanses of whiteness and ice. *(Photo Credit for Mo anchoring: Vincent Moeyersoms)*

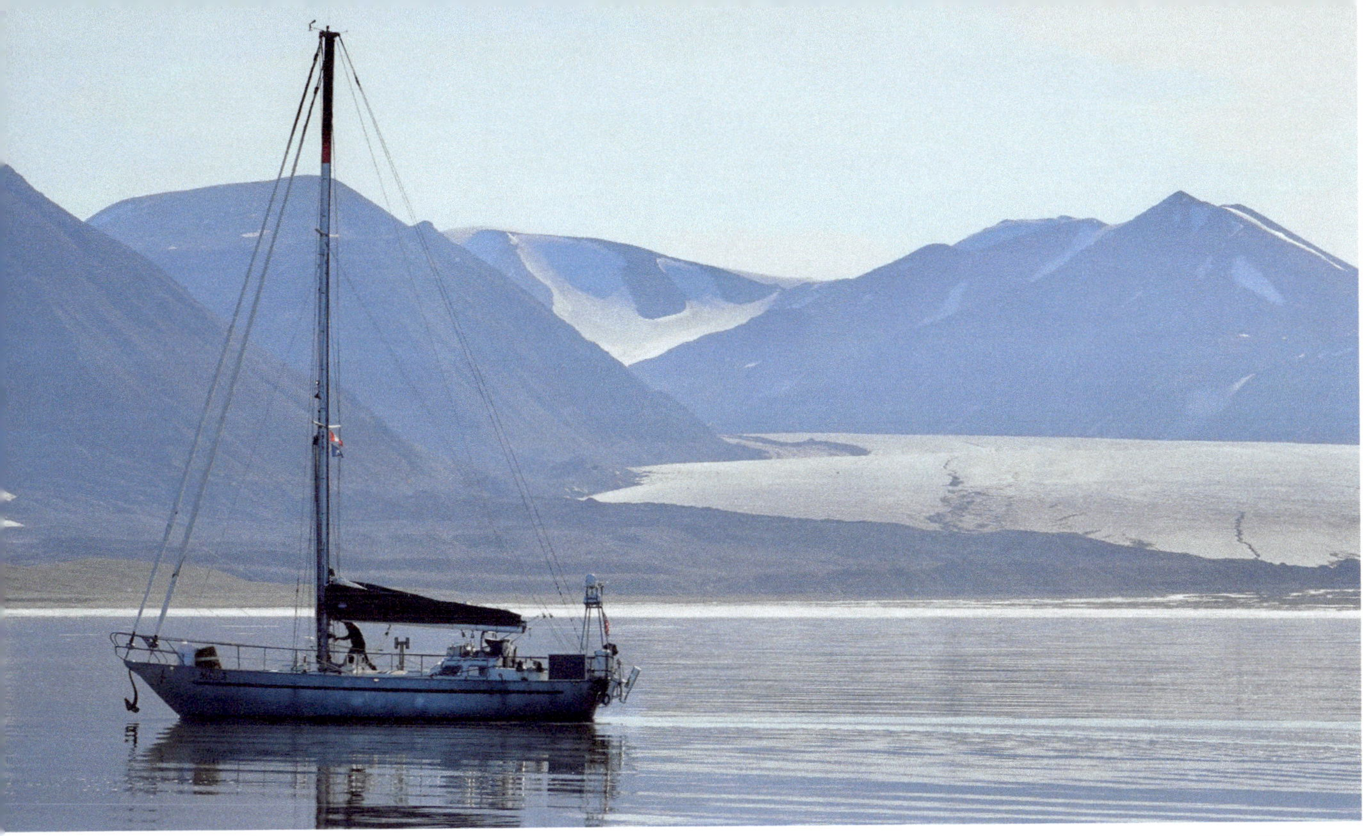

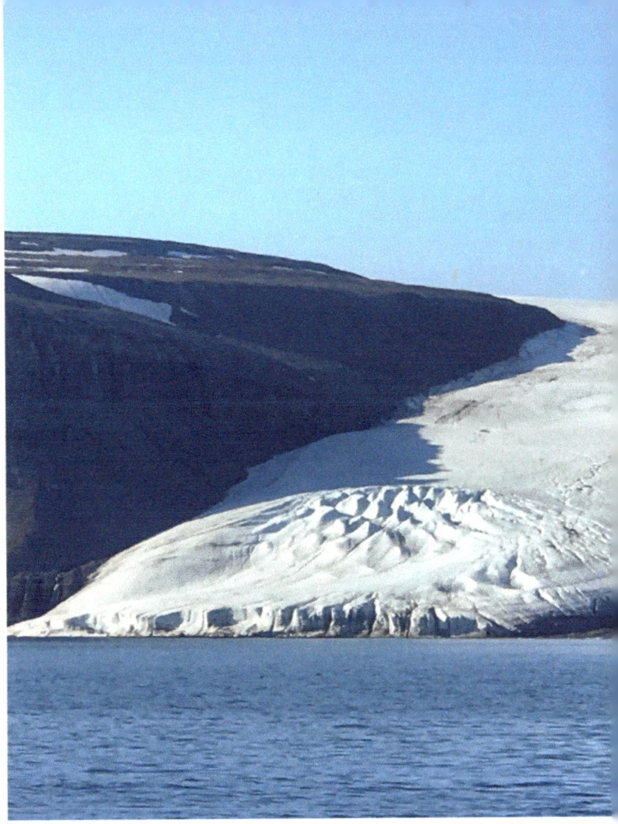

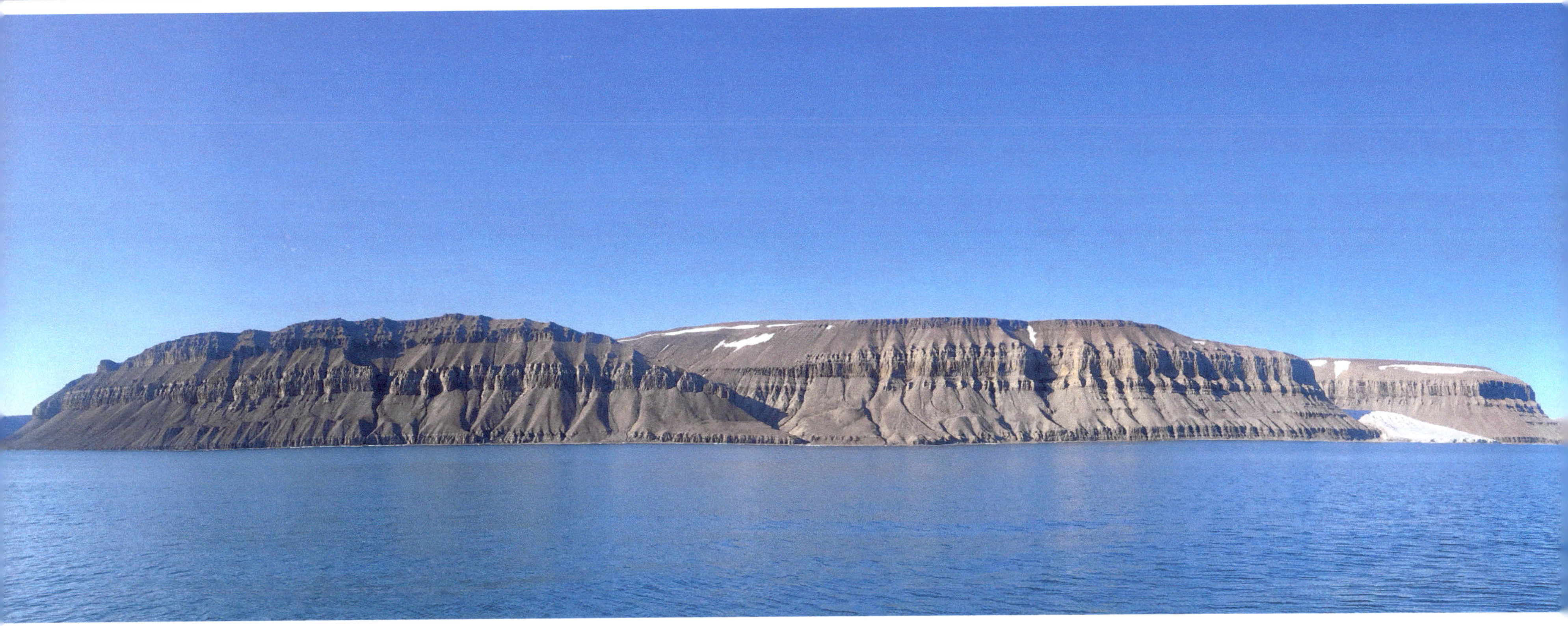

Top: **August 17, day 321.** *Mo* and I begin to encounter denser pack ice as we turn south into Peel Sound. For now, the days are sunny and calm and perfect for making way through these fields of sharp and jagged teeth. But there are many miles to go and what we will find further on is unknown.

This page: **Finding time for sleep** in the Northwest Passage is a challenge. Working through ice requires that I hand steer *Mo* for many long days, stealing a nap here and there as conditions allow. Once when I was particularly fatigued, I dashed below and set the alarm for a brief, five-minute nap as *Mo* made her way through an area of what I thought to be open water. On the fourth minute of that nap, the boat collided with a bergy bit the size of a truck and came immediately to a dead stop. Fortunately, though dazed, stout-hearted *Mo* continued on unhurt.

This Page: **August 20, day 323.** Below the Tasmania Islands, *Mo* and I joined company with a Belgian yacht named *Alioth*, whose transmission had failed in the heart of the year's worst ice. The skipper, Vincent, requested we be *Alioth's* consort for the last leap to the south. They would have to sail out, and we could be an extra set of eyes during the thick of things. When we made it, three cheers were exchanged between boats. Later, and when the wind died, *Mo* was able to offer tow for the final miles to Cambridge Bay, which allowed both boats to reach safety before the onset of an intense summer gale. (*Photo Credit: top left and facing page: Vincent Moeyersoms*)

*Above: **Alioth's** crew of three—* Vincent, Olivier and Jean—ran a smart and comfortable ship, which included the daily baking of fresh bread. As we exited the ice, *Alioth* closed *Mo* and tossed over a still-warm loaf, whose receipt was better than gold.

*Left: **Station attendants*** in Cambridge Bay fill *Mo's* jerry cans while the waiting line grows.

Above left: **Two old boats** decorate the beach of Cambridge Bay.

Above: **Two Sandhill Cranes** make their way north.

Bottom right: **The fueling pier** near the Northern Store in Tuktayotuk.

Bottom left: **In Tuktoyatuk** is one of the many Distant Early Warning (DEW) Stations that mark the Northwest Passage route.

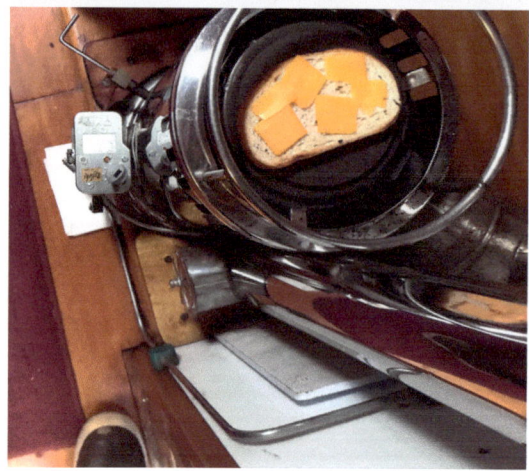

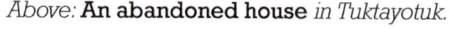

Above: **An abandoned house** *in Tuktayotuk.*

Below: **Toasting bread** *and cheese on the diesel stove.*

Facing page: **The majestic cliffs** of Cape Lisburne in the Bering Sea.

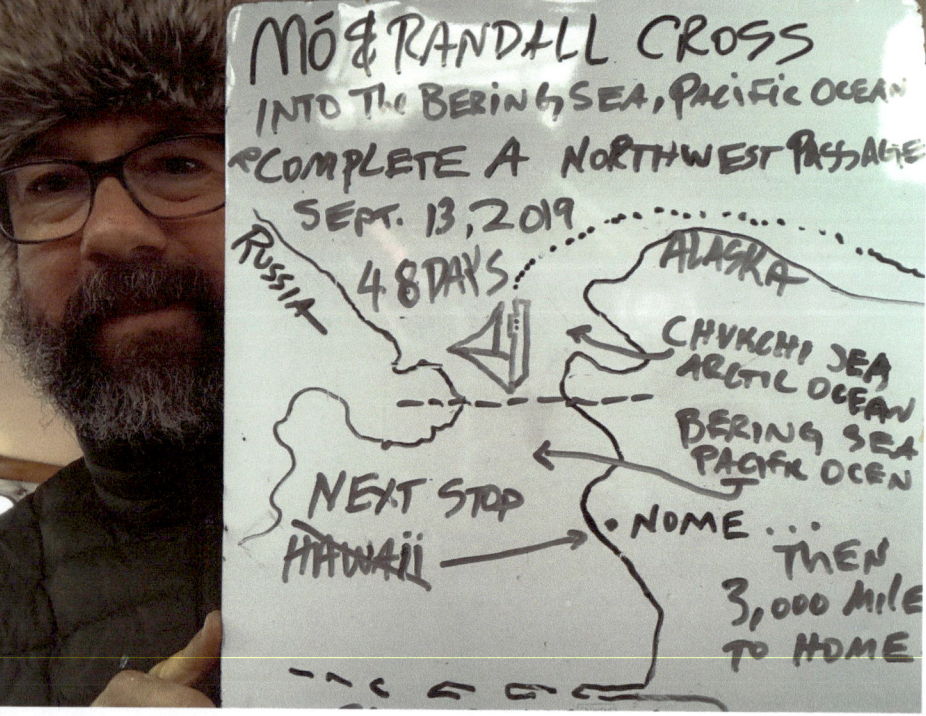

MO & RANDALL CROSS
INTO THE BERING SEA, PACIFIC OCEAN
*COMPLETE A NORTHWEST PASSAGE
SEPT. 13, 2019
48 DAYS

RUSSIA

ALASKA

CHUKCHI SEA
ARCTIC OCEAN

BERING SEA
PACIFIC OCEAN

NEXT STOP
HAWAII

NOME...
THEN
3,000 MILE
TO HOME

Left: **September 13, day 349.** *Mo* arrives Nome, Alaska just after midnight on her seventy-second day out of Halifax, Nova Scotia.

Top: **Pictured are the Northwest Passage crews** of *Morgane*, *Mirabelle* and *Alioth* as we all celebrate a successful year in the Arctic.

Below: **Stopping for a photo** with the bust of Roald Amundsen.

Above left: **From Nome,** we soon headed south so as to stay ahead of winter. A brief touch in Dutch Harbor and a midnight threading of Akutan Pass, and with that *Mo* and I were back into the vast Pacific on our last reach for home.

Above: **Brisk southerlies** persisted for a week, driving us toward the Oregon coast. Then as *Mo* and I were on final approach, a northerly gale brought with it the most difficult seas we'd seen since Halifax.

Facing page top: **Regal Point Reyes emerges ahead.** Within the hour we are around the green entrance buoy and then it's time to rig the anchor. It had been just over a year since we weighed from this very bay for the start of the Figure 8 Voyage, and now we had returned from our long road. One task remained, to sail the last few miles to San Francisco and home.

October 17, 2019 *Mo* is anchored in Drake's Bay upon her return from the Figure 8 Voyage, having sailed 39,048 miles in her quest to circumnavigate the Americas and Antarctica in one season.

Homecoming

October 19. After 384 days away, today *Mo* **and I would sail under the Golden Gate Bridge. Today we would be coming home.**

From the log…

5am. The alarm sounds to wake me though I've been up since three o'clock. For some time I lay in the dark listening to the wind whine in the rigging. *Mo* tugs at her chain. I wait for sleep to descend again, but it has slipped away in the night to play with the coyotes calling from the headland.

Today we return home. My heart pounds. The bunk rejects me.

I make coffee but can't sit to drink it. By flashlight I continue the endless job of tidying the deck in preparation for our Golden Gate entry.

6am. A pale dawn silhouettes the mountains. We are underway for the Golden Gate Bridge. During these final jaunts, I have been worried the engine will fail or the windlass will quit and that I will be forced to enjoy the ignominy of a tow. But Big Red fires as usual; the anchor picks clean.

I point *Mo* to the southeast and toward Limantour Beach, well clear of the Chimney Rocks reef. Yesterday, we encountered a long, large swell from the NW. At Point Reyes and over this reef, seas stacked up frighteningly. Giants curled and crashed and leapt for the lighthouse. At the reef, their break extended well past the green buoy. Without a moon, I can't see them now, but I can hear the roar of white water. *Mo* passes through billows of spume and rolls deeply.

9am. Motoring in flat calm. The morning is drippy. A high fog flows from the north as we pass Duxbury Point. These will be my last hours alone with *Mo*, and I feel an urge I can't define. Not to be out to sea again, but an agitation. We've nearly run our course. A thing I have ardently desired is imminent. Do I desire it now?

Right: **Negotiating a lumpy sea** over the San Francisco bar just beyond the Golden Gate Bridge. *Mo* and I had arrived too early and were forced to wait for the turn of the tide. *(Photo Credit: Heather Richards)*

At Mile Rocks, we will be joined by other vessels that will sail us in. At Cavallo Point, family and friends will be waving. At the Sausalito Yacht Club, I will encounter other friends and the press. Closure and an opening, but an opening to what?

There is a sense of foreboding, not at the idea of being home but rather at the display that will accompany my return. Will I be what people expect? Will I remember my remarks? Will I make a sailing blunder for all to see?

Having passed so many difficulties, having relied so often on my own resource and on *Mo's* extraordinary ability and still to be worried about what others will think. It appears I have not left my faults behind. *"What we have done, we have done,"* I say in my own defense.

10:30am. I am an hour early to Mile Rocks. Already there are three boats waiting and two climbing the light west wind from the Gate. Congratulations are shouted across the water as we heave through the swell on the bar. Now there are ten boats, including friends who sailed out to see me off a year ago. Slowly I let

the wind and tide draw us closer to the gate. Red rocks, red bridge, gray sky. Now there are fourteen boats in the flotilla. Horns blast as we slide below the great span, and then we are in the bay. For years I have followed the track of the Figure 8, always pressing on and pressing further, and now the double loop is finally closed.

12:30pm. I let *Mo* take the wind on the beam and we race toward Cavallo Point. One last charge. Show them what you can do, my friend! Then a cheer at the point as we swing round. Waves and cheers and the flood pulling us further in.

Then we are nosing into the yacht club. A bagpipe sounds. Hands reach for lines. Other hands catch *Mo's* rails. Gently she is eased into the dock. Another cheer for Mo. Joanna approaches smiling. A kiss for completion. In that instant we have pierced the veil.

We are home.

Above: **Entering under the bridge** in company with a small flotilla of friends, many of whom had sailed out to see me off the year before. *(Photo Credit: Heather Richards)*

Top right: **Being met at the Sausalito Yacht Club** dock by Joanna, friends, and the media. *(Photo Credit: Caron Shahrestani)*

Above right: **Greeted by a kiss from my wife,** Joanna, as bagpipes play in the background. *(Photo Credit: Caron Shahrestani)*

Above: **Waving to family and friends,** who'd come to welcome us home. What a pleasure to see faces I'd not seen in a year. *(Photo Credit: Mike Wilcox)*

Facing page, top right: **Joanna had presented me with this rose gold ring** strung from a ribbon the day I departed with the words, *"You must bring this back to me."* In more ways than one, I was pleased to oblige. *(Photo Credit: Caron Shahrestani)*

Above: **Good friend,** former owner of *Moli* and mentor, Tony Gooch, presenting me with a plaque of congratulations from the Ocean Cruising Club. (*Photo Credit: Caron Shahrestani*)

Top right: **Friends and family** gather on the deck of the Sausalito yacht club. (*Photo Credit: Caron Shahrestani*)

Right: **My mother, Evon Reeves,** looking much happier than the day I departed. (*Photo Credit: Caron Shahrestani*)

Far right: **Signing autographs** for some boys at the rendezvous. What an honor. (*Photo Credit: Mike Wilcox*)

About *Moli*

Moli was built by the firm Dubbel and Jesse in Germany in 1989 for adventurer Clark Stede, who named the boat *Asma* and, with Michelle Poncini, circumnavigated the Americas between 1990 and 1993.

Her next owners, Tony and Coryn Gooch, renamed the boat *Taonui* and cruised for years in high latitudes. Then in 2002, and aboard *Taonui*, Tony was the first to complete a non-stop, solo-loop of the globe via the Southern Ocean from a starting point in western North America. In 2013, *Taonui* passed to Ann and Glenn Bainbridge and became *Gjoa* for another east-to-west transit of the Northwest Passage that terminated in Homer, Alaska where, in 2016, she became *Moli*.

Clark Stede and Michelle Poncini on the Northwest Passage. *(Photo Credit: Clark Stede from* Rund Amerika*)*

Mo is ideally suited for high latitude expeditions with short-handed crews. Her hull is strongly constructed and features three watertight bulkheads. The long keel adds stability at sea and helps protect the aft hung rudder and propeller from ice and other entanglements. Her deck arrangement, including tiller steering, a small cockpit, oversized winches and a large but simple sloop rig, means she is easy for one person

Asma **under sail** in the Caribbean, 1992. *(Photo Credit: Clark Stede from* Rund Amerika*)*

to manage. Below, her ample fuel tankage and small engine give her great range under power, and equally large water carry means she can avoid the needless complexity of a watermaker. All in all, *Mo* was the perfect machine in which to make a Figure 8 Voyage.

Tony Gooch below Cape Horn, 2002. *(Photo Credit: Tony Gooch)*

BUILDER: Dubbel and Jesse, Norderney Germany

YEAR BUILT: 1988/1989

MATERIAL: Aluminum

KEEL: Full with cutaway forefoot

LENGTH OVERALL: 44 feet

BEAM: 12 feet

DRAFT: 6 feet

BALLAST: 8,000 pounds

DISPLACEMENT: 35,000 pounds

ALUMINUM PLATE
KEEL: 10mm

BELOW WATERLINE: 8mm

ABOVE WATERLINE: 6mm

RIG: Twin headsail sloop

ENGINE: Bukh diesel, 48 horsepower, keel-cooled

TANKAGE: Two hundred gallons of diesel in two pilothouse tanks; two hundred gallons of water in two keel tanks

---

STEERING: Tiller to Monitor windvane or autopilot guided by satellite compass

Left: **Asma** **in build** at the Dubbel and Jesse yard, Norderney, 1988. *(Photo Credit: Clark Stede from* Rund Amerika*)*

Top: **Taonui** **and Tony Gooch** headed around the world, 2002. *(Photo Credit: Tony Gooch)*

Above: **Gjoa** **on the hard,** Cambridge Bay, Arctic Canada, 2015.

Not Entirely Alone

It should be no surprise that a solo enterprise of this scope will require the help of many. Though the voyage was simple in concept, the execution necessitated aid from family and friends, a great number of counselors and vendors, and people I'd never met who simply wanted to be involved.

Wherever we stopped for rest or repairs, in Ushuaia, Hobart, Halifax, St. John's, Nuuk, and in the Northwest Passage, there people materialized to lend a hand with a job or a lift into town or a dinner out.

My special gratitude to those who provided key resources, Tony Gooch, Gerd Marggraff, Dustin Fox and Victor Wejer; to Eric Mathewson

at WideOrbit, Paul Kaplan and the team at KKMI, Mike Scheck, Suzy, Ross and Ichiro of Monitor, Robin Sodaro at HOOD Sails, Marjorie Goux at Clif Bar, and Pam Wall; to Nick and Cherry Stewart for Figure 8 inks and artwork and for the design of this book.

I am particularly appreciative for support from the many listed below…

Virtual Voyagers Who Supported the First Figure 8 Voyage attempt:

Jim Walter, Mike Dodson, Jim Major, Ian Griffin, Susie and Lon Woodrum, Jeremiah "JJ" Kosten, Peter Weady, Sarah Carlisle, Franklin Delfgaauw, John Woodworth, Joel Brown, Mary Wildavsky, The Milham Family, Emily Baxter, Lavonna Reeves and Bruce Jahnke, Robert Bellah, Doug Soderstrom, Mark Caplan, Jeremy Barry, Sally Lomax Mallet, David R Kelton, Johnny Ceritto, Ben Markowitz, Dale Bagwell, Lucy & Matt Heston, Stacy & Schubert

Sarkis, Ryan Floyd, Michael Berry, Mary Beth McClure, Merriman and Eric Mathewson, Quincy & Mitchell Andrus, Katherine Ott, Colleen LaFontaine, Jane Huxley, Maria Sipka, Steve Sullivan, Elisa Camahort Page, Caryn King, The Metal Boat Society, Emily McLanahan, Chris Gould, Stacey de Larios, Erin Rand, Stephanie Eidelman, Tom Shields, Lorraine Hendrickson, Lawrence Killingsworth, Jonathan Green, Sarita Jha, Gina Diaz, Jessica Shor, Harriet Bates and Family– Shani Higgins, Elizabeth Dean, Kim Le,

Stewart McDowell, Denise Brosseau -- Maria Fernandez, Tony Gooch, Laura Marino, Nancy Bush, Annie Rogaski, Richard Herman, David Norris, Jeremiah Kosten, Shelby Joy Scarbrough, Mickey Wilson, Kurt Lorenz, Colleen Blake, Ambra Wellbeloved, JD Burch, Ann & James Shepherd Rozzelle, Shannon Stubo, William Estep, Ben Shaw, Debbie Frank, Andrew Coward, Joan Fallon, Burt Richardson

Virtual Voyagers Who Supported the Second Figure 8 Voyage attempt:

Guy Reeve, Arthur Gregory, Peter Haeussler, Skip Dubrin, Rhiannon and Sebastiaan, Samuel Johnson, Ryan Floyd, Linda Newland, Kevin Giffin, Dave Blankenship, Kurt Hafferman, David Hipschman, Nan Shellabarger, Skip Dubrin, Calvin Holt, Kurt Hafferman, Michael Miles, Regan Wieland, Paul Stoner, Michael La Guardia, Bill Gallagher, Skip Dubrin, Derek Lundy, Tim McDonough, Richard Mackie, Mike Luxton, Troy and Barb Lutz, Daniel Lee, Claude and Evelyn Solanas, Paul Troy, Anthony Allen, Raymond Frato, Harald Bjerke, Skip Dubrin, Denis

Sinyakov, Kathy Lund, Annemieke Van der Werff, Ryan Floyd, Bill Nork, Susie and Lon Woodrum, Westsail Tortuga, Harald Bjerke, Brian Lockett, Teunis BAAS, Diana Lauer, J Michael Rice, Pierre LaRochelle, Harriet Bates, Jeremy Barry, Mark Caplan, Janis Johnson, Mary Wildavsky, Yaron Levite, Lucy Heston, Carmen Campbell-Hewitt, Jaime and John Surenkamp, Shana Chrisman, Amy Chandler, Paul Goc, David Arthurs, David Norris, C Daniel Smith, Mary Spadaro, Arthur and Vera Tertyshny, Barry Hutton, Benjamin Shaw, Mark Godden, Schubert

and Stacy Sarkis, Sally Lomax, Paul Eisfeld, Benjamin Markowitz, Michael Berry, Mike Dodson, Lawrence Killingsworth, Sidney Shaw, Kurt Lorenz, Andrew Coward, Brian Russel, Guy Erb, Teresa Wilcox, James Murphy, John Martin - Robb Jones, Tony Gibb, Jorge Bermudez, Michael Scipione, Chuck Fulton, Jeffrey Wettig –Gina Catalano, Phil Genera, Jim Walter, Howard Conant, Scott Smith, Mary Francis, Robin White, Bruce Allen, Paul Scheuerman

Those around the world who generously gave of their time:

Homer, Alaska: *Adam Lalich, Mike Stockburger and the Homer Boat yard, Eric Sloth of Sloth Boats;* **Port Townsend, Washington:** *Howard and Stephanie Conant and Cory Armstrong;* **Honolulu, Hawaii:** *Nikolai Maximenko, Jan Haffner and Mary Spadaro;* **Ushuaia, Argentina:** *Roxanna Diaz, Laura and Federico of Ocean Tramp;* **Hobart, Tasmania:** *Captain John Solomon, Darryl Ridgeway and Ursula, Sally Errey, John and De*

Deegan and the crew of John Barleycorn; **Halifax, Nova Scotia:** *Wayne Blundell, Rob Kuder, Sandy MacMillan, John van S, Rich of Wabi, Sebastiaan Ambtman and Rhiannon Davies, Ben Garvey, John Harries, Tony Gibb and Connie McCann;* **St. John's Newfoundland:** *Ted Laurentius, Jerry Veitch, Alisdair Black, Dennis Hanlon, Ed, Greg Horner and Rick Austin;* **Nuuk, Greenland:** *Jens Kjeldsen;* **Sisimiut, Greenland:** *Mantas Seskauskis;*

Northwest Passage: *Victor Wejer, Vincent Moeyersoms, Olivier and Jean; Olivier Huin, Eric, Leila and Josh of Breskell; Pablo and Pablo of Mandragore; Amanda and Robin of Morgane; Anton, Guillom, and Elouise of Mirabelle;* **Ocean Cruising Club:** *Roxanna Diaz, Captain John Solomon, Jon Van S, Ted Laurentius, Rick Whiting and Daria Blackwell.*

The Figure 8 land ops team: *Kylie Teele, Freddy Bunkers, Lauren Pfenninger, Brad Kellar, Lucy Bloor;* **The arrival, flotilla media logistics team:** *Heather Hawkins, Daria Blackwell, Heather Richard, Mike Dodson, and Gary Pursell, and the Sausalito Yacht Club;* **For early exposure:** *Charles Doane, Matt Rutherford, Tim Henry, Andy Schell, Ben Shaw, Joe Rosato Jr, Jeffrey Wettig.*

To Family: *Evon Reeves, Lavonna Reeves and Bruce Janke, The entire Vietz, Kellar, Shaeneman, Bloor, Carlisle and Bates families; especially Jessie Vietz;* **And to Friends:** *Kelton Rhoads, Jim Walter, Matt Jensen Young; Kurt Lorenz; Bill Gallagher; Joan Fallon, Mike Kayton, Lawrence Boag, Ben Shaw and Lauren Keane, Eric Moe, Schubert and Stacey Sarkis, Skip Dubrin, Bruce Allen, John Woodworth, Diane Hayford and Joe Geary, Mary Spadaro, Mike and Mickey Wilson, Shana Chrisman, Tony Gibb, Connie McCann and Deirdre McGlashan.*